RYA

INTRODUCTION TO PERSONAL WATERCRAFT

RYA
INTRODUCTION TO PERSONAL
WATERCRAFT

JakeKavanagh

RYA Introduction to Personal Watercraft
Copyright RYA 2006
Revised By Paul Mara 2006

The Royal Yachting Association
RYA House
Ensign Way
Hamble
Southampton
SO31 4YA
Tel: 0845 345 0400
Fax: 0845 345 0329
E-mail: publications@rya.org.uk
Web: www.rya.org.uk

ISBN 1-905104-12-X
ISBN 978-1-905-104-12-3

RYA Order Code G35

Telephone 0845 345 0400 for a free
copy of our Publications Catalogue.

Totally Chlorine Free

Sustainable Forests

EMAS
VERIFIED
ENVIRONMENTAL
MANAGEMENT

Art director **Simon Balley**
Design **Balley Design Limited**
Designer **Tom Morris**
Illustrator **Rob Brandt**
Cover Design **Balley Design Limited**
Cover PW **Kawasaki Motors UK**
Typeset **Balley Design Limited**
Proof reading and indexing **Alan Thatcher**
Printed in China through **World Print**

contents

welcome to the water

Personal Watercraft are exciting craft that, when used responsibly, offer a great deal of enjoyment and fun. As manufacturers are producing bigger and more sophisticated machines the sport is developing into a family pastime. There are many clubs around the country that organise events from treasure hunts to extended cruises. Whether you are new to the sport or an experienced PW user this book will be the perfect companion to perfecting your skills leading to more enjoyment out on the water. This book is also the perfect companion for the RYA Personal Watercraft course, covering the syllabus and much more.

Paul Mara
RYA Chief Powerboat Instructor

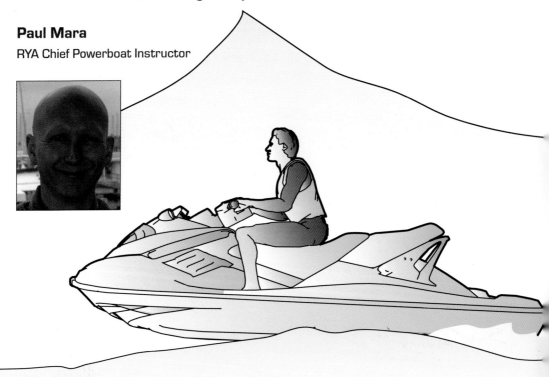

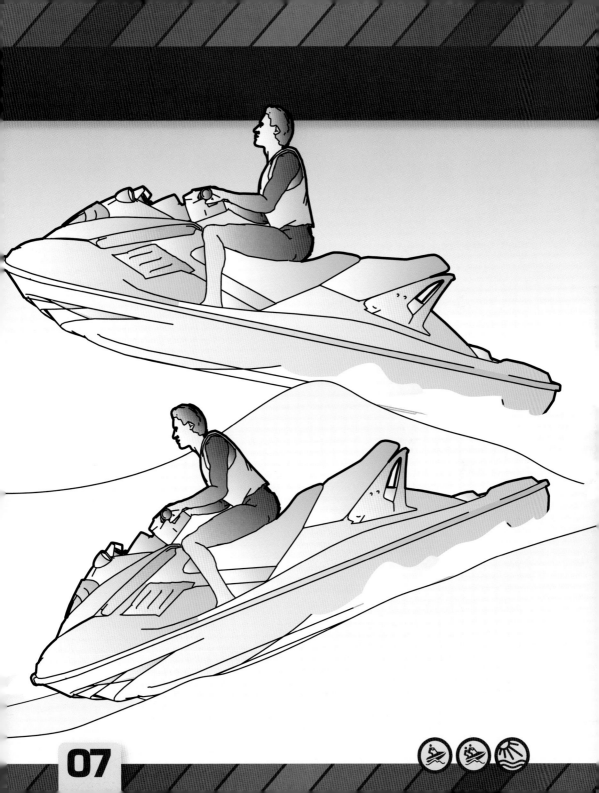

personal watercraft course syllabus

The One Day Personal Watercraft Course covers the topics set out below and is usually taught in the order shown, however, the order may be changed due to local conditions or the weather on the day.

Instruction ashore

Introduction
❯ Layout of a PW; controls; propulsion and steering system; fuel and oil; stowage compartment
❯ Personal equipment, wet suit/dry suit, personal buoyancy, head and eye protection
❯ Pre launch checks
❯ Essential safety information. Kill-cord, safe speed, local hazards.

Collision Avoidance
Rules of the Road applicable to PWs, including:
❯ Lookout
❯ Safe speed
❯ Priorities between different classes of vessel.
❯ Overtaking, crossing and end-on approach rules.
❯ Local Rules, speed limits, prohibited areas.

Orientation at sea
❯ Charts, scales, direction and distance
❯ Representation of land, shallows and deep water. Buoys, lateral and cardinal, avoiding shipping channels, special buoyed areas for water skiing etc, tides, high and low water and tidal streams.

Weather, Safety, Courtesy to other water users
❯ Sources and significance of weather forecasts.
❯ Lee and weather shores
❯ Safety and emergency equipment
❯ Courtesy to other water users
❯ Avoiding pollution and disturbance and damage to wildlife habitats.

Instruction afloat

Launching and Familiarisation
▸ Launching from a trailer; boarding in shallow water and starting the engine.
▸ Control at slow speed. Balance and trim.
▸ Falling off and reboarding. Capsizings and rightings.
▸ Control at speed. Stopping distances.

Orientation
▸ Following a planned route, identifying buoys and marks.

Collision avoidance
▸ Recognising potential collision situations and taking correct avoiding action.

PW control at speed
▸ Slalom exercise

Emergencies
▸ Towing a PW - knots: bowline, round turn and two half hitches.
▸ On completion of this practical exercise, recovering the PW from water and preparation for trailing and storage.

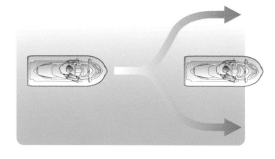

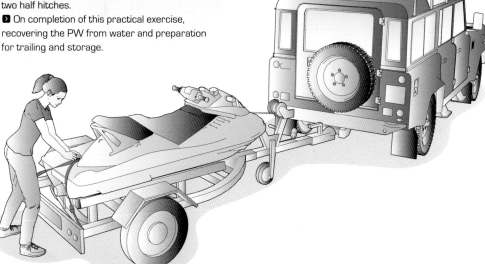

types of pw

Designed by a motorcycle-mad Texan, a Personal Watercraft is best described as a boat powered by a waterjet but with an enclosed hull; sometimes called wetbikes, or Jetskis although Kawasaki copyrighted the latter as a trade name.

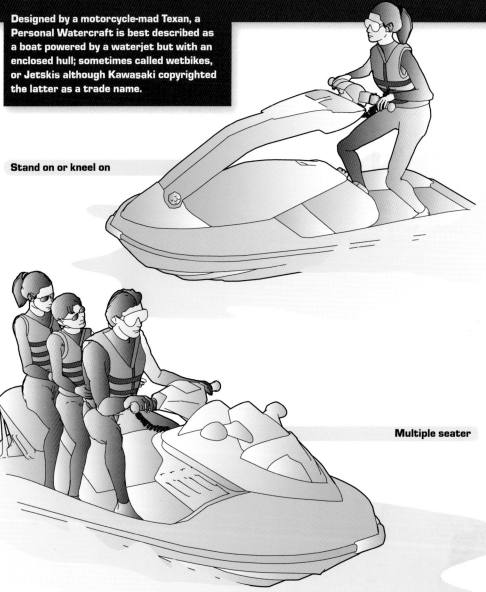

Stand on or kneel on

Multiple seater

How it works

▸ Water is drawn into the chamber and squirted out again under pressure, rather like placing a thumb over a garden hose. The direction of the jet is controlled by the handlebars, so that the craft can be steered.

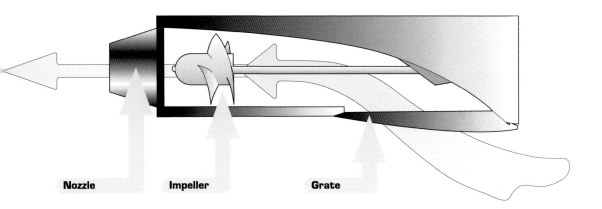

Nozzle **Impeller** **Grate**

At rest **Displacement** **Planing**

Planing hull

▸ A PW has a planing hull.
▸ The flat bottom and spray rails provide lift and the PW skims the surface. Below planing speed, they are displacement boats, and create a sizeable wash.

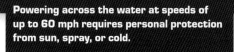

personal gear

Powering across the water at speeds of up to 60 mph requires personal protection from sun, spray, or cold.

A buoyancy aid will help keep you afloat.

Dry suits

❯ Dry suits are ideal off season or in cooler climates, but need to be worn with a base layer. Don't rely on the suit's buoyancy - wear a buoyancy aid or life jacket as well.

❯ Squeeze the excess air out of the suit before you go afloat or trapped air may cause you to float at an uncomfortable angle.

Wet suit

▶ Many types and styles are available. Look for a snug fit preferably with an alloy zip. The short sleeved types are only suitable for warm weather conditions.

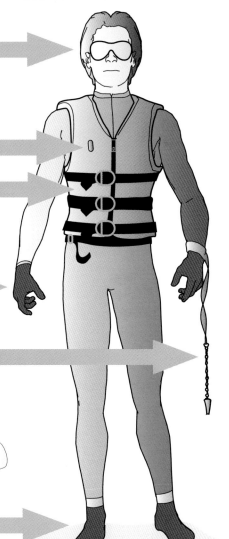

Goggles

Spray stings and the water reflects a lot of glare. Wear special PW goggles, or place goggles over your sunglasses or prescription glasses.

Whistle

To attract attention.

Buoyancy Aid

An essential bit of kit which should be a minimum of 50 Newtons and, ideally, a specialist PW buoyancy aid designed to be impact resistant. Many will have a strong point for the attachment of the kill-cord.

Gloves

To help grip wet controls.

Kill cord

To stop the engine if you fall off. These are often coded, to act as a security device as well. Make sure it has a strong connection to your clothing or wrist.

Sun Block

A few minutes on a PW with reflected sun and windburn is the equivalent to several hours on the beach.

Foot protection

Needed for a good grip on the footrests. Useful during launch and recovery.

layout and controls

Before using your PW for the first time, read the manual and familiarise yourself with the controls and routine maintenance schedule. Some manufacturers supply a DVD or video. Remember, Americans do things slightly differently, especially when it comes to navigation marks.

1. **Stop/start button**
2. **Variable Trim System switch** - (optional)
3. **Speedometer** - a guide only
4. **Kill cord attachment** - stops the engine if you fall off
5. **Choke**
6. **Reverse gear** - (optional)
7. **Fuel switch**
8. **Fuel gauge**
9. **Throttle**
10. **Seat** - (removable to get to engine underneath)
11. **Tell-tale outlet for rooster trail** - (some models only)
12. **Grab handle**
13. **Towing eye**
14. **Mirrors**
15. **Fuel tank**
16. **Exhaust**
17. **Battery**
18. **Engine**
19. **Bucket reverser** - (optional)
20. **Oil tank**

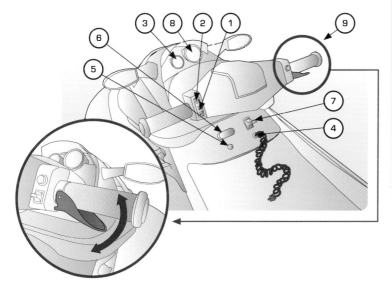

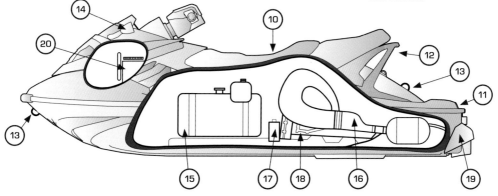

nautical terms

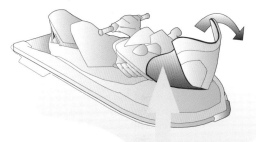

Watertight storage

PWs have a watertight compartment for stowing gear.

Engine

▶ With advances in 4 stroke technology most new PWs come with a 4 stroke engine. The advantages of this are they are quieter, more economical and have more environmentally friendly emissions. Remember however some machines have two stroke engines with separate tanks for petrol and oil that are mixed automatically.

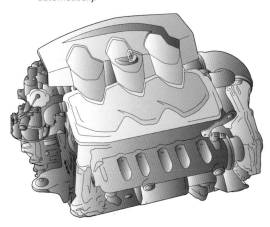

Parts of the ski

▶ Port and Starboard refer to the boat as seen from the helm (driver) looking forwards. Starboard is always the right side of the craft, port is always the left.
▶ Anything behind the helm is usually described as aft.

Port

Bow

Starboard

Helm

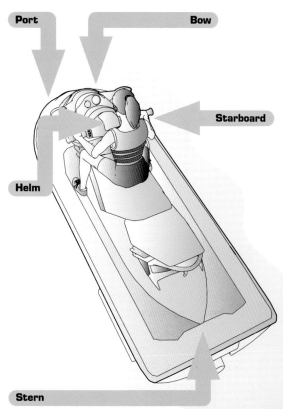

Stern

essential gear

1. Fire extinguisher - (2kg)

2. Flare pack - recommended minimum is one pinpoint red and two orange smoke

Mini-flare packs - fit onto the buoyancy aid and are useful for attracting attention if you are separated from the craft.

3. Torch - for signalling

4. Knife with serrated edge

5. Food and drink

6. Documentation - some local authorities insist on a permit and proof of insurance, and have patrol boats that carry out checks.

Cash - you may end up some way from your car

7. 5 metres of 8mm nylon rope - for towing, securing to a mooring, or anchoring.

8. Small first aid kit

9. Small grapnel anchor which folds flat

10. Tool kit and spare spark plugs

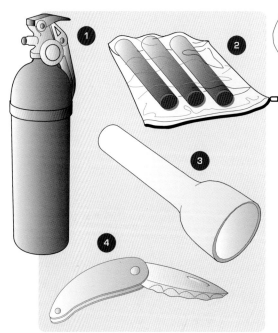
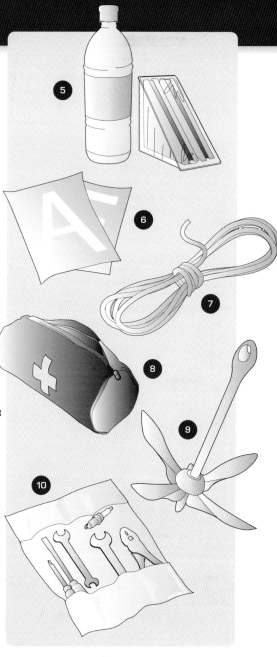

pre-departure checks

- Is your trailer legal? Remember the speed limit; it's 50mph (60 on motorways)
- Check trailer tyres, they work at different pressures to a car.
- Is PW use permitted?
- Is there a slipway?
- Do you need a licence?
- Are there any restrictions?
- Is the PW fully fuelled?
- Do you have enough fuel for a full day out?
- Is the weather forecast OK? When is high and low water? It will help with launching to know.
- Check controls are free, and the throttle is smooth. Salt water is very corrosive and may cause damage.
- Check the hull for damage.
- Is all the gear aboard?
- Is the battery OK? PW left standing may need a battery boost. Take the battery off the machine when charging, as it might damage the systems.

Trailer tips

- Keep the nose down. Bring the strap downwards before it goes onto the winch. This will give added security to the load by holding it firmly onto the trailer.
- Before attaching the light-board to the trailer, place it alongside the driver's door and work the foot-pedals and indicators. You can see at once if you have a problem with any of the lights. Wrap spare cable around the trailer to stop it dragging on the ground and shorting out.
- Don't put straps across the machine. This can distort the hull. Use the ring provided at the back.

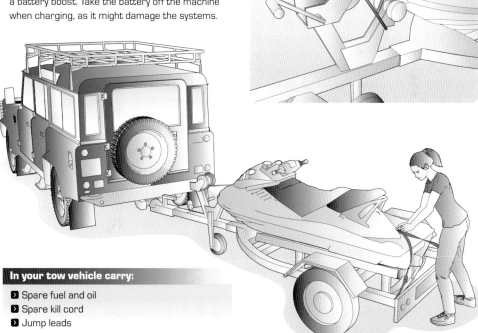

In your tow vehicle carry:

- Spare fuel and oil
- Spare kill cord
- Jump leads

17

pre-launch checks

Avoid hassle by checking local weather conditions before taking to the water. Visit the local harbour office, ask the beach warden or the local boat or PW clubs.

❯ Check local bye-laws. Is a permit required? Is there a charge for the slipway?
❯ Some authorities require a number to be displayed on a PW.
❯ Park the car well above the high water mark.

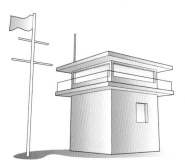

❯ Use a torch to check the impeller. Make sure no road debris has found its way into the chamber.
❯ Test start and stop the engine once on the main switch, and again using the kill-cord. (Note - in built up areas several PWs test running out of the water can cause a noise nuisance. Start the PW before setting out, and start when immersed, but before leaving the trailer.) Check that no one is behind you when you test it.

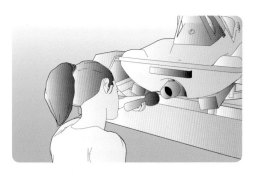

❯ Check the controls and hull again in case of damage in transit.
❯ Remove straps and number board (People do forget!)
❯ Make sure the bung is in, or your trip will be a short one!
❯ Check engine compartment for any oil or fuel leaks. Mop up any spillage and dispose of it properly.

Get dressed for action

❯ Before launching ensure that everyone going on the water changes into their wetsuits etc.

❯ Study the launch site. Watch other users to see which way the tide is flowing, how steep is the slipway? Where can the craft be secured after launch? Other water users or harbour staff will be able to offer advice.

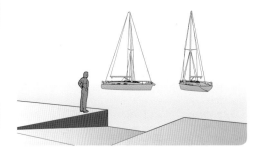

launching

If you're new to using a trailer, practise first. Reversing is the area where most people have trouble as the trailer steers the opposite way to the wheel. Practising will save time and frustration on the slipway which may get busy at weekends.

Slipways and hards vary

▶ Some are excellent at all states of the tide, some stop abruptly below the water, others are cratered, some end in thick mud. Try and get some local knowledge if you are unsure.

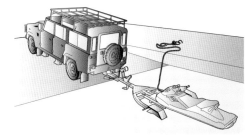

Single handed launch

▶ Attach a long line to the PW so that it can be pushed off of the trailer into deeper water. You can use this long line to either pull the PW to the back of a jetty or harbour wall. Keep the kill cord with you when you park your car to prevent theft. If left on the concrete slip the underwater hull may get damaged by waves from passing boats. Always secure craft, rising tide may lift a beached one so that it drifts away.

Two handed launch

▶ Rider mounted with buoyancy aid securely on, killcord connected and pre-launch checks completed. PW can now be pushed off into deeper water. Try to get the machine pointing in the direction you want to go. Use reverse, if you have it, to get off the trailer.

Shallow slipway

▶ On shallow slips the car exhaust pipe may become immersed in the water before the PW is properly afloat. To avoid this, attach a long line to the trailer and with rider mounted push it out into deeper water. The trailer can then be recovered by securing the rope to the hitch.

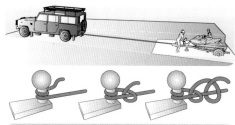

Round turn and two half hitches

And off you go

▶ Rider starts the engine and motors slowly away.

Trailer tip > When you arrive have a ten minute break before launching to allow the bearings in the wheels of the trailer to cool down. Hot bearings suck the cold water past the rubber seals and into the bearings, shortening their lives.

Climbing aboard

1. PWs are quite tippy, so when boarding from a jetty, try and place your weight across the machine.

2. In shallow water, board from the rear, keeping your centre of gravity low.

3. As soon as you are on board attach the kill cord. From a beach try not to operate the engine in less than 3ft of water, slowly motor into deeper water so the pump does not pick up sand or gravel and sling it at other beach-users. Stones will make short work of your impeller and require expensive repairs. In shallow water, watch out for weed, proceed slowly, varying the throttle to avoid entanglement.

4. Make sure you haven't left a mooring line trailing in the water.

5. Look out for the swimming area, often marked with buoys or flags on the beach. Waves will hide bobbing heads from sight. Beaches with designated swimming areas will have a buoyed channel to take you safely offshore. Get well away before speeding up.

6. Keep an eye on your fuel - use ⅓ going out, ⅓ coming back, keep ⅓ in reserve.

7. Harbours have speed limits. Stick to them. 1 knot is slightly more than 1mph - 6 knots = 7mph. Don't trust your speedometer (or log), which may be unreliable at low speeds. In harbour areas go no faster than a quick walking speed.

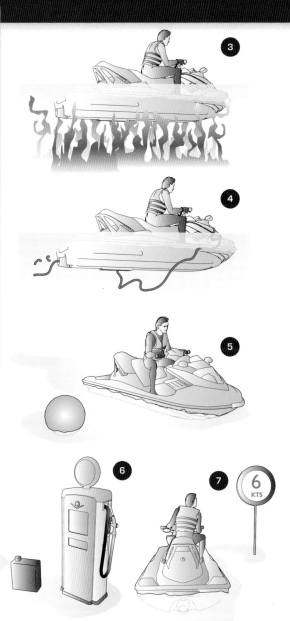

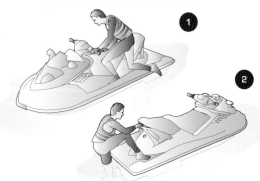

basic steering and trim

Underway

1. The jet drive relies totally on the waterjet to steer. Remember, no throttle - no steering.

2. A burst of throttle will turn the craft with very little forward momentum. There's no clutch or gearbox.

3. Some PWs have a clamshell arrangement, so they can reverse by deflecting the jet. This is not a brake, you'll rip it off if you try to use it like one. Use reverse only at low speeds. The clamshell may also have a neutral position.

4. Some PWs have a variable trim mechanism.

5. Trim down will get you on the plane quicker, especially if you have a passenger. Trim up will lift the nose, useful in choppy water.

6. The PW relies on water resistance to stop. Come off the power at speed and see how long it takes the machine to come to a halt. Try throttling down at various speeds - you'll need to know how long it takes to stop when approaching a beach, you will have to stop the engine before reaching the shallows.

7. The PW can be stopped quickly by a radical change of course.

8. If something appears in front of you, a hard turn with full throttle will flip the machine out of the way. Coming off the power will simply mean you run into the object. Remember, you need throttle for thrust and steering.

9. If you are unfamiliar with your PW, take your first few rides in a quiet area. Practise turns, capsizing and recovery in water close to the shore.

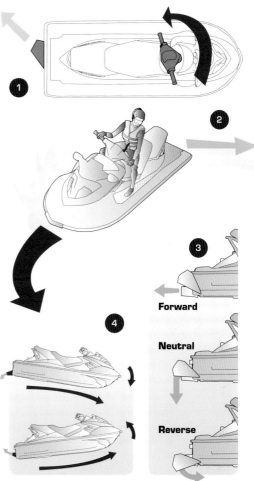

Forward

Neutral

Reverse

Remember > You need throttle for thrust and steering. If something appears in front of you, a hard turn with full throttle will flip the machine out of the way. Coming off the power will simply mean you run into the object.

capsize

PWs are designed to turn over, it can be part of the fun. Always keep your buoyancy aid done up with the kill cord attached to your wrist or a strong point on your buoyancy aid.

After capsize

- Make sure the engine has cut out.
- Check the label on the stern for the way to rotate the craft. You can damage the engine if you rotate it the wrong way.
- Swim alongside, put one hand on the grille and one on the grab-handle. Put toe (or knee) on rubbing strake if possible.
- Roll the craft over so the water drains off. Move to the stern, climb over the back, do not tread on any of the jet parts, it may cause damage.
- Keep body low as craft is unstable, especially in choppy water.
- Re-attach kill cord. Restart without choke but with slight throttle.

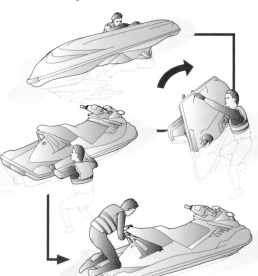

Capsize with passenger

- Check the passenger is still with you and uninjured.
- Keep passenger in sight, roll the craft upright. Passenger should hold craft and help keep it steady.
- Climb over the stern as before, assume the driving position. Once seated and balanced, ask passenger to follow.

Restart machine

- If engine does not restart the carbs may be flooded with fuel - leave it for a few minutes.
- If it still won't start don't try to effect repairs out on the water.
- The open engine hatch will unseal the machine, and it could be sunk by a capsize.
- Get a tow, but first make sure you agree there is no fee. Someone could tow it in and claim salvage. Stay with the machine. Don't let it drift.

rules of the road

It is vitally important to know what to do if a collision looks likely. Try to make your reactions instinctive and always remember that the other driver may not know what action to take. Assume it's up to you to avoid a collision.

Lookout

- Keep a proper lookout
- Most collisions are caused by failure to see an approaching vessel in time.

Remember > Maintain an all round lookout, don't just look at the water ahead.

Priorities

- You will probably be faster and more manoeuvrable than anything else afloat. The rules require that more manoeuvrable boats keep clear of less manoeuvrable ones.

You must give a wide berth to

1. Dredgers
- and other working craft which are unable to manoeuvre

2. Fishing boats
- Even if they don't appear to be fishing they could have booms out each side, or submerged tackle.

3. Sailing boats
- can only go where the wind will let them.

4. Boats operating with divers
- Divers often surface some distance from their mother ship. Look for the international signal of a white and blue flag.

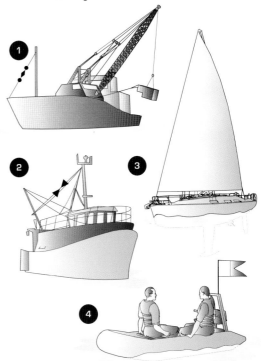

You should keep clear of

1. Canoeists and rowers
▶ Canoes are very low in the water and can be very hard to see, they can capsize in waves. Rowers face backwards when rowing so give a wide berth to both.

2. Large vessels, especially ferries
▶ Supercats are massive versions of your PW. Don't play chicken with them - if you fall off in the turbulent wave and get sucked into their intakes, you're human puree.

3. Commercial shipping
▶ Stay well away from all commercial shipping. It takes a long time for them to stop their propellers - that's if they can see you!

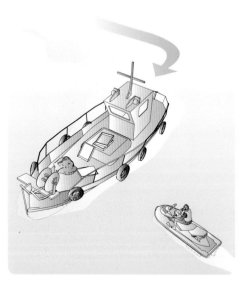

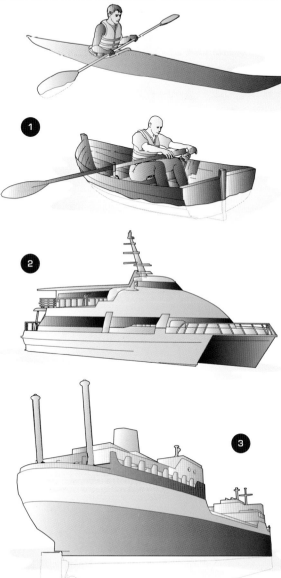

Fishing boats are experts at sudden changes of course when recovering their gear.

Head to head

▶ Always turn to the right if a collision looks likely. Make the turn EARLY and OBVIOUS. You can't signal with hands, otherwise you'll come off the throttle, but you can signal with your entire PW. If in doubt, slow down or stop.

▶ Throughout the world, at sea, head on collisions are avoided by both craft turning to the right.

▶ If you can't go right (restricted channel - marina entrance) stop and signal the other vessel through.

▶ On the water drive on the right.

In open waters

▶ You only have to turn right if a collision looks likely.

▶ In narrow channels, always keep to the right (starboard) hand bank, irrespective of which way you are going.

> **Remember >** Right is right. Give way to the right, turn to the right. Think - RIGHT

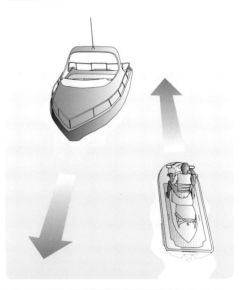

Sound signals

Boats often use sound to signal their intentions. If you hear a boat hooting at you, don't be offended, they are just communicating.

■ **One short blast** - I am altering course to starboard. (Turning to their right)

■■ **Two short blasts** - I am altering course to port (Turning to their left)

■■■ **Three short blasts** - My engines are going astern. (Often used by ferries and water-taxis backing out of a berth into the main channel)

■■■■■ **Five short blasts** - Your intentions are not understood. In other words, Look Out!

Most PWs are unable to make a sound signal in return.

CROSSING: This one always causes confusion, but just think of it as a roundabout where you have to give way to the right.

Crossing from right to left

- You must give way.
- Alter course to go behind him. Do it early. Make it Obvious.
- Remember the yield zone.
- If in doubt slow and stop.

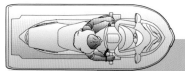

yield zone

Crossing from left to right

- Now he has to give way - but watch him - he might not know the rules!
- Be prepared to slow down or stop if he holds his course or speed.
- Don't turn to port (left), in this situation it could make matters worse.

Remember > It is down to the vessel to avoid a collision, if in doubt slow down and allow the other boat to pass.

Overtaking

▶ In open waters, you can overtake either side, but stay well clear. The other driver may not have seen or heard you, and could suddenly swing in front of you.

Look out

▶ Always glance over your shoulder before altering course. Someone may be about to pass you. A good ALL ROUND lookout saves lives.
▶ Don't trust the PW mirrors - they're normally covered in spray. USE YOUR HEAD, - THINK.

Safe speed

▶ In the open sea there is no precise speed limit in mph but the rules say that speed must be moderate.
▶ Don't go fast near swimmers, where there are large groups of boats, in narrow channels, or close to beaches.
▶ Watch out for the speed limit signs in harbours.

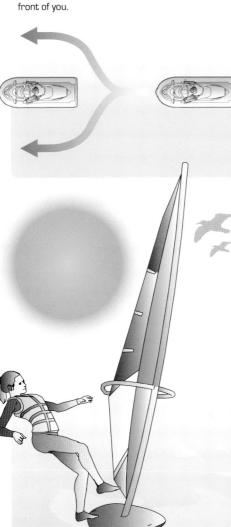

buoyage

▶ This is how the buoys and beacons should look when entering a harbour.

Red light

Red

Green light

Green

1. Isolated Danger Marks - Danger with safe water all around
2. Safe Water Marks - Safe water
3. Special Marks - Special marks can mean: anything from a deep channel to a swimming area (Check a chart for details).

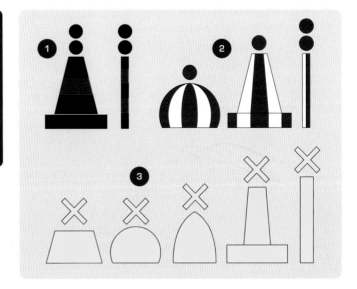

▶ The cardinal system is based on the points of the compass. Each mark tells you which side to pass it to avoid danger.

north

▶ North cones point up.
Keep to the north.

west

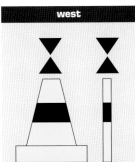

▶ Some people remember west top mark as a bobbin to "wind wool' or as a W on its side. **Keep to the west.**

DANGER

east

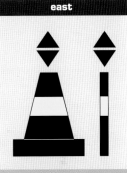

▶ An east top mark can be likened to an egg.
Keep to the east.

south

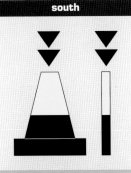

▶ South cones point down.
Keep to the south.

29

inshore waters

Throughout Europe, the buoyage is positioned for boats to find their way INTO a harbour. Buoys that mark a well defined channel are called lateral marks, and are identified by shape and colour. Keep the can shaped reds (port hand markers) on your left and the cone-shaped greens (starboard hand marks) on your right when coming in.

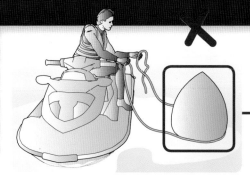

Look for landmarks

▶ Remember to check over your shoulder as you leave an unfamiliar harbour or beach. You'll have to find your way back again. Look for a conspicuous coastal landmark. Entrances to harbours are often hard to find. Memorise the way home.

▶ It is often safer to navigate just outside the main channel to avoid large ships.

Do not tie up to navigation marks

Points to remember

▶ Buoyage takes you INTO a harbour. Reverse it for coming out.

▶ Buoys or top marks are shaped so you can still identify them in poor light or glare.

▶ Come home with the cones.

Take a chart with you.

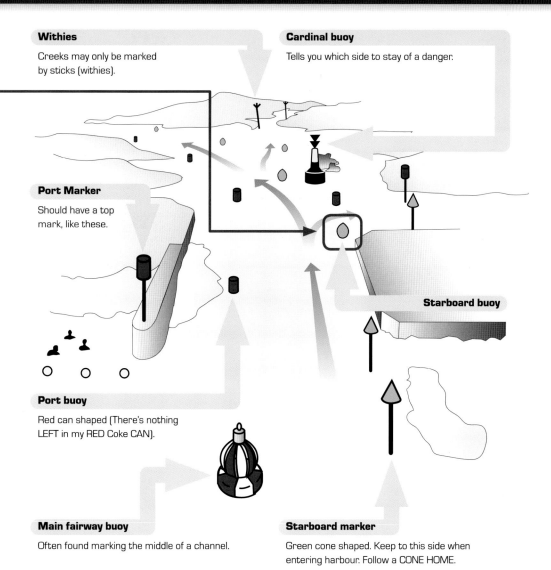

Withies

Creeks may only be marked by sticks (withies).

Cardinal buoy

Tells you which side to stay of a danger.

Port Marker

Should have a top mark, like these.

Starboard buoy

Port buoy

Red can shaped (There's nothing LEFT in my RED Coke CAN).

Main fairway buoy

Often found marking the middle of a channel.

Starboard marker

Green cone shaped. Keep to this side when entering harbour. Follow a CONE HOME.

further offshore

If using your PW in an unfamiliar area or making a passage along the coast, you need to carry a chart. Study it before you go to see if there are any off-lying dangers. A PW is a vessel, and just as vulnerable to coastal hazards as any other vessel. Treat the sea with respect.

❯ If using your PW in an unfamiliar area or making a passage along the coast, you need to carry a chart. Study it before you go to see if there are any off-lying dangers. A PW is a vessel, and just as vulnerable to coastal hazards as any other vessel.

❯ Treat the sea with respect.

❯ If you are going into unfamiliar waters, carry a compass and a chart and check on the tides and tidal streams for the day.

❯ A chart is a nautical map, showing all the things you would find on a land map and a lot more besides.

❯ A Small Craft Admiralty Chart, obtainable from most chandlers, can be wrapped in a special waterproof sleeve.

❯ Carry a compass, a divers wrist type is suitable to help you navigate.

❯ Fog is common off the coast at certain times of year, including high summer, and without a compass you can be totally lost within minutes.

❯ Longer passages are best made in company with other boats or PWs which can provide support in the event of engine breakdowns or any other difficulties.

❯ Leave details of your intended expedition with someone ashore. These details should include your intended route and destination and the time at which you expect to complete the expedition. Give your shore contact a call when you arrive or if you call off the expedition. Many hours of rescuers' time are wasted looking for people who are safe ashore but haven't made contact with relatives at home who are worried about them.

❯ The weather might be fine when you set out but will it be like that all day? Check the weather forecast and make sure that the wind speed is not predicted to increase or the visibility to drop. PWs don't mix with very strong winds or fog, so be prepared to put off your plans until a more suitable day.

❯ For longer trips a marine VHF radiotelephone is a very useful aid to safety.

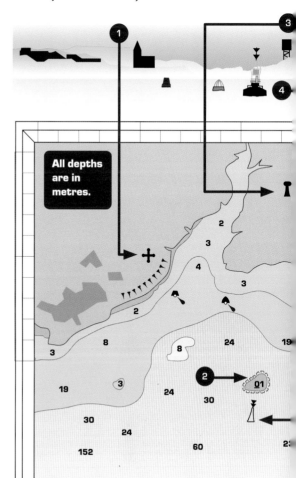

All depths are in metres.

1. Church
2. This is a drying height, and shows an area that dries to a height above chart datum, the lowest possible low tide.
3. Water tower

4. A cardinal buoy. These buoys tell you which side to stay (North, South, East or West) to avoid danger.
5 Ship Mooring Buoys
6. Lighthouse

7. Wreck
8. Radio Mast
9. A headland. Off-lying shallows can create vicious overfalls.
10. Isolated danger mark

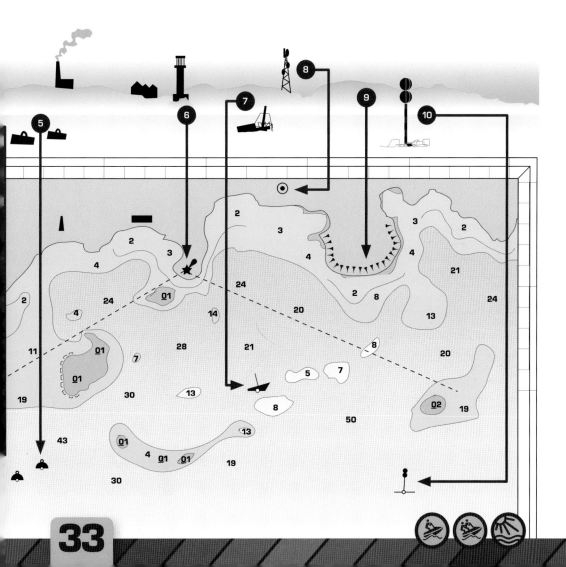

safety and emergencies

The safest way to go to sea is with another PW, so there is another craft to assist if you break down. Make sure you have a length of rope with you or the other craft won't be able to help.

VHF Radiotelephones

> A marine band VHF radiotelephone allows you to talk direct to the Coastguard and to other boats at sea.

> If you are going on long trips it is worth having one but you will need a radiotelephone operator's certificate and an annual licence for the set. Details of courses for the operators certificates are available from the RYA.

Towing

> When towing, attach the line to a towing point with a bowline. Your helm will provide some steering, but keep the speed fairly low. Remember, the towing vessel will use more fuel than usual.

> If on your own, attracting the attention of other craft will be the biggest problem. If you are broken down but not in any immediate danger, try waving or beckoning to any passing boat.

Visual Distress Signals > In a serious situation, when you think you will be in grave danger and need immediate assistance you can use one of the internationally recognised distress signals:

Arm Movements

> Up and down outstretched arms. (Note: Do this very slowly, as fast arm movements are little more than a blur at any distance.)

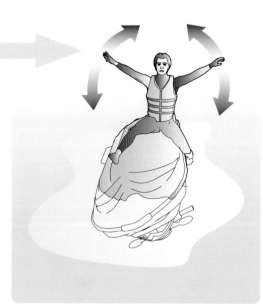

Flares

▸ If you are really in danger do not hesitate to call for help - delay could be fatal in deteriorating weather conditions or when night is falling. But you must not use a distress signal if all you want is a tow back to the shore on a calm day and there are plenty of other boats or PWs around who could help.

▸ In bright sunlight the most effective signal is an orange smoke flare. In dull, overcast conditions a red hand-held flare is visible from further away. Don't use all your flares at once, keep one in reserve to pinpoint your position when you can see a lifeboat, helicopter or other rescuer.

Mobile phone

▸ Kept it in a waterproof bag. A mobile phone can be used to raise help close to shore. Dialling 999 or 112 from a mobile phone will raise the Coastguard; an emergency service. Be sure to tell them the nature of your emergency and exactly where you are because, unlike VHF transmissions, your position cannot be established from a mobile phone call. Mobile phones were never designed to go to sea, don't put your faith entirely in them. Keep the battery fully charged.

tides and tidal streams

The UK and Atlantic coasts have some quite impressive tides, unlike the almost non - tidal Mediterranean. In some areas, the difference between high and low water can be as little as 1 to 2 metres, but in others such as the Bristol Channel it can be as much as 12 metres. As a general rule, the tide rises and falls roughly once every twelve hours, six hours to come in and six hours to go out. The time of high water advances by about 50 minutes each day. The height of the tide is governed by the phases of the moon. At Spring tides, which happen every two weeks, high tide will be higher and low tides lower; at neaps, the other two weeks, tidal differences are more moderate. What the tide is doing will affect how near the slip you park your car and where you launch and recover the PW.

Tidal stream

Wind

Tidal stream

❱ As well as going up and down, the whole body of water moves sideways - six hours in one direction and six hours in the other. This is known as a tidal stream. In river estuaries and harbour entrances the incoming tide floods in and then ebbs out. In a narrow entrance, the tidal stream can reach speeds of up to 10 knots.

❱ You can usually tell at a glance what the tidal stream is doing.

❱ Boats moored to buoys will usually face into the tidal stream.

❱ Buoys and other fixed objects will create a tell tale wake.

❱ Be aware of tides in your area. A very low tide may make recovery difficult.

❱ The tidal stream can carry a disabled PW away very quickly possibly at speeds of up to 6 mph. Carry safety and survival gear on board at all times.

❱ Wind with tide will have a calming effect.

❱ Tide tables can be found at the harbour office, in nautical almanacs and at chandlers.

❱ Tidal streams against wind can create short, sharp and confused seas.

Reading a tide table

❱ Tide tables show the times and heights of high and low water. The heights are given in metres above chart datum which is the lowest the water will ever go.

wind and waves

Personal watercraft can handle roughish seas, but you need to be an expert and it is very tiring. Should you be caught out in a squall, or if conditions deteriorate more than anticipated, try to read the waves. Throttle back at the crest otherwise the pump comes out of the water. Trim up to lift nose slightly. Fuel will be used much more quickly with constant throttle changes. Stand up PWs may find it easier to punch directly into the waves.

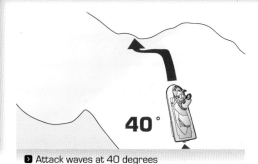

▸ Attack waves at 40 degrees

▸ Both wind and tide accelerate around headlands. Expect to find rougher seas here

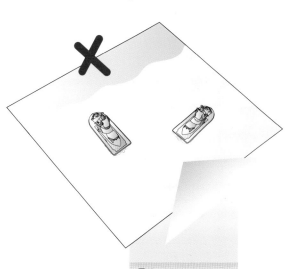

▸ Avoid a lee shore

▸ Power on... off... and on again

Rough water is fun, but re-boarding a capsized craft will be particularly difficult.

local regulations

PWs have been targeted by many local authorities for special attention. PWs are not toys, and require both physical maturity and experience of judgement. Under 16s may not be allowed to drive a PW unaccompanied.

SMALL CRAFT CHANNEL

PW 0313

▶ A number of local authorities will request a permit and insist that the craft carries a number on the bow.

▶ Some busy commercial harbours have special channels to keep Small Craft out of the way of shipping. Some harbours have a ban on PWs altogether.
▶ Many harbours have no-go areas usually to protect endangered wildlife. Stay away from these areas.

Look out for warning signs such as >
1. Personal watercraft zone high visibility marker
2. 10 knot speed limit marker buoy
3. 10 knot speed limit
4. Personal watercraft activity prohibited
5. Personal watercraft permitted

courtesy to other water users

▶ Don't rev-up in shallow beach areas - you will spray beach-users with sand and gravel.

▶ Noise travels easily across water, especially in hot, still weather. Using a PW in one area all day will annoy others.

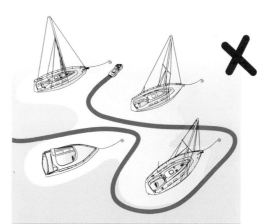

▶ Don't wave jump behind a boat. Fun though it is, the close proximity of a PW can be unnerving and irritating. There are plenty of waves to jump at sea. Stern hogging boats is a nuisance and dangerous.

Don't weave in and out of an anchorage

▶ Don't weave in and out of an anchorage at high speed. Your tell-tale can spray others.
▶ You may fail to spot people swimming around their boats. Keep the high speed stuff away from anchored boats.
▶ Avoid areas where there are swimmers. If close inshore, drop to displacement speeds and maintain a good lookout.

sources of weather information

Weather forecasts are available from many sources including radio, television and weather charts posted outside harbour offices.

Force 1

▶ The shipping forecast including the forecast for inshore waters is broadcast every day on Radio 4 at 0535 (FM and Longwave), 1201 (Longwave) 1754 (Longwave-weekends FM also) and 0048 (FM and Longwave). Wind speeds are given using the Beaufort scale.

▶ Forecasts will also give an idea of visibility. Fog is the greatest threat to an offshore PW because they have no electronic navigation aids and drivers can easily become disorientated.

Force 2

The PW Beaufort Scale for open waters.

Force 1. Wind speed 1-3 knots. Just ripples on a smooth sea. **Perfect weather for a long distance run.**

Force 2. Wind speed 4-6 knots. Small wavelets, not breaking.

Force 3. Wind speed 7-10 knots. Gentle breeze. Large wavelets, crests beginning to break. Wave height about 1 ft. **Beginners will struggle.**

Force 4. Wind speed 11-16 knots. Small waves growing longer. Fairly frequent white horses. **Experienced hands only.**

Force 5. Wind speed 17-21 knots. Fresh breeze. Moderate waves taking a more pronounced form. Many white horses, perhaps some spray. At the top end of PW driving. **Hardened experts only. Very tiring and becoming very dangerous.**

Force 6. Wind speed 22-27 knots. Strong breeze. Large waves forming. White foam. Crests more extensive. Forget it. **Put the PW away for another day. You'll only break it.**

Force 7 - 11. Definitely do something else.

Force 3

Force 4

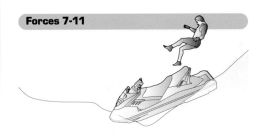
Forces 7-11

knots, anchoring and towing

Knots

You only really need to know two knots to use a PW.

1. Bowline - a good strong knot useful for towing or anchoring.

2. Round turn and two half hitches - to attach lines to the tow hitch for shallow launching.

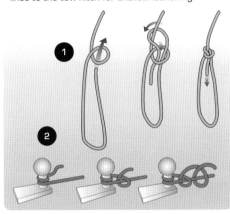

Anchoring

▶ The anchor line attaches to the winch eye on the bow.

▶ Using the small grapnel anchor and a 5m length of rope, a PW can be safely anchored in shallow water.

▶ Make sure the anchor is securely on the bottom, if it's not your PW will float away. A careful eye needs to be kept on it, as a rising tide can make the anchor less effective. Alternatively, a bag full of stones can be used.

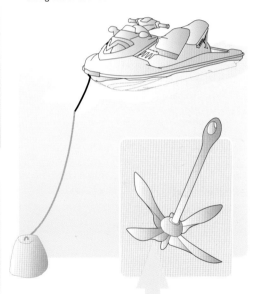

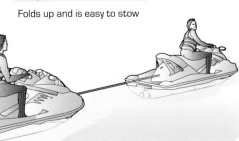

Grapnel Anchor

Folds up and is easy to stow

Towing

▶ Use a bowline for towing a PW. Keep the towing speed to a minimum, no faster than a brisk walking pace, water can be forced into the engine if the towing speed is too high. The owners' manual will tell you how to close off water intakes if a long tow is anticipated.

▶ If a larger vessel comes to your aid, they may be able to take your PW aboard.

▶ Before accepting help from another vessel, check that they are not going to make a claim for salvage against you. It's unlikely, but some individuals will offer you help and, when your PW is recovered, demand part of its' value, expecting your insurance company to pay up. Agree terms before you accept the tow-rope.

water skiing

Many multiple seater **PWs** are capable of towing a skier but, as with any motor vessel, must follow the safety regulations, most of which are plain common sense.

Learn the internationally recognised hand signals to communicate with your skier.

Faster

- All powerboats (includes PWs) towing water skiers should be occupied by two competent persons, a driver and an observer. The driver can concentrate on the water ahead, whilst the observer can pass on the skier's signals.
- Tow boats should be operated sensibly at a safe distance from people and property. Recklessness or deliberately endangering people is stupid and potentially fatal.
- Water-skiing before dawn or after dusk is dangerous. Good visibility is required at all times.
- When operating at sea or on a large expanse of water, the waterskier should wear a buoyancy aid.
- Keep well away from swimmers and swimming areas, which will be marked with yellow buoys.
- Tow lines of floating line are normally not longer than 75ft.

Turn right

Faster

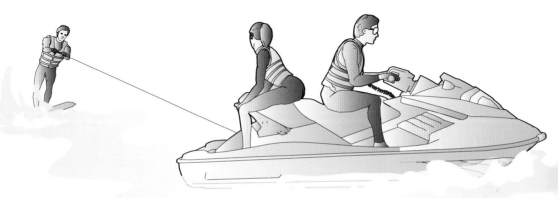

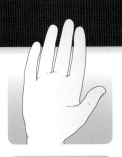

Stop

Turn around

Slower

Slower

Stop

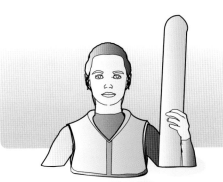

Skier down - stay clear

Back to dock

I'm OK

recovery from the water

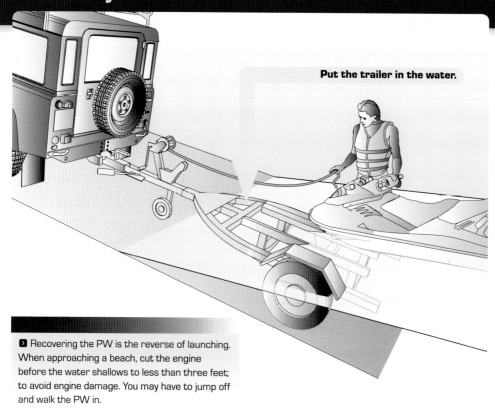

Put the trailer in the water.

▶ Recovering the PW is the reverse of launching. When approaching a beach, cut the engine before the water shallows to less than three feet; to avoid engine damage. You may have to jump off and walk the PW in.

▶ It is best practice to winch the PW onto the trailer rather than ride it on. Hands can get trapped between the bow of the PW and the winch, and misjudgment under power could seriously damage your machine and cause serious damage.

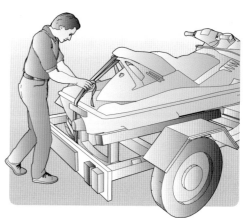

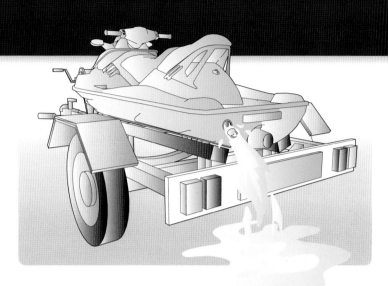

▶ Make sure the craft is securely attached to the trailer before pulling it out. Once clear of the water; attach a freshwater hose (if available) to the special flushing intake (see owners' manual). Start the engine before turning on the water supply. Run for a few minutes to force the salt water from the system. Switch off the water and expel any water left in the system by giving a short burst of the throttle, finally switch off the engine.

▶ If it's a residential area, this may be better done at home, as several PWs purging at once will create a nuisance. You don't want a petition going around to have the slipway closed to Personal Watercraft.

▶ Attach and test the lightboard by laying it alongside the car before re-attaching. Check straps, and check all seats and hatches are properly closed for the journey home.
▶ Wet suits and other gear can be washed in a mild detergent in the bath.

unacceptable risks

While highly manoeuvrable and versatile, PWs are vulnerable to the same dangers as other craft.

1. Riding whilst intoxicated is a short cut to disaster. Balance, vision and judgement are all affected. Alcohol and high performance boats of all types do not mix.

2. Avoid fog. The PW will give a feeble (if any) radar return, and could easily be run down by another vessel.

3. Avoid travelling at night. Even with navigation lights, which any powered vessel must carry during the hours of darkness, the PWs small profile makes it vulnerable. A drifting PW will be even harder to spot.

4. Avoid breaking water and tidal rips. In these conditions a capsized PW could easily be swept onto rocks, or caught in undertows which will make reboarding impossible.

Don't drink and ride.

aftercare and maintenance

Salt water is very corrosive, so putting your PW into storage without flushing it through with fresh water will result in quick deterioration of metal components, especially in exposed areas such as the throttle cable.

Top tip > When flushing with freshwater start the engine before the water. After flushing the reverse applies - stop the water before the engine.

After use at sea

▶ Thoroughly wash the outside of the PW down with fresh water and a mild detergent so all the salt is removed.

▶ Connect the cooling inlet to a freshwater hose via a proper adapter and run the engine for a couple of minutes to wash through all the salt. (If no cooling water is available, do not run the engine for more than a few seconds.)

▶ Remove the seat and sponge down the inside of the engine bay.

▶ Whilst sponging out, check for oil leaks, or anything that may have worked loose during the day's play. It doesn't hurt to tweak up hose connectors.

▶ If the PW is stored under cover, this will prevent condensation from building up. Partially replace the seat, allowing the engine bay to vent out.

▶ Open the forward storage area, sponge out and allow to dry.

▶ Follow the owners' handbook, and lubricate any moving parts as directed. Areas to pay particular attention to are the throttle cable and moving parts of the drive. It is important to use lubricants recommended by the manufacturers, as many car products are mineral based and react badly with sea-water, setting up electrolysis in your PW and causing increased corrosion.

▶ For longer term storage, remove the battery, take out the plugs, add two-stroke oil into the cylinders and reattach the plugs loosely. Your authorised dealer will give your PW a full winter lay-up service.

▶ Look after your PW, and it will look after you.

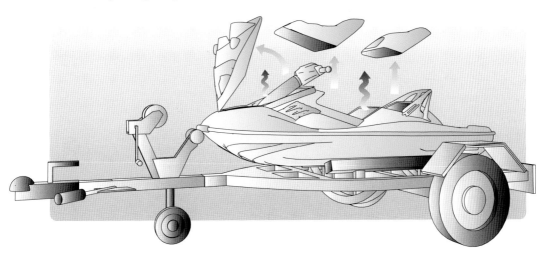

Index

RYA *Membership*

Promoting and Protecting Boating
www.rya.org.uk

RYA *Membership*

Promoting and Protecting Boating

The RYA is the national organisation which represents the interests of everyone who goes boating for pleasure.

The greater the membership, the louder our voice when it comes to protecting members' interests.

Apply for membership today, and support the RYA, to help the RYA support you.

Benefits of Membership

- Access to expert advice on all aspects of boating from legal wrangles to training matters
- Special members' discounts on a range of products and services including boat insurance, books, videos and class certificates
- Free issue of certificates of competence, increasingly asked for by everyone from overseas governments to holiday companies, insurance underwriters to boat hirers

- Access to the wide range of RYA publications, including the quarterly magazine
- Third Party insurance for windsurfing members
- Free Internet access with RYA-Online
- Special discounts on AA membership
- Regular offers in RYA Magazine
- ...and much more

Join now - membership form opposite

Join online at *www.rya.org.uk*

Visit our website for information, advice, members' services and web shop.